A HELEN EXLEY GIFTBOOK

≣EXLEY
NEW YORK • WATFORD, UK

ANYTHING, EVERYTHING,
LITTLE OR BIG
BECOMES AN ADVENTURE
WHEN THE RIGHT PERSON
SHARES IT.

KATHLEEN NORRIS
(1880-1966)

A husband makes you feel special by telling you that no one is going to hurt you while he's around. He makes you feel unbelievably precious, which is the most wonderful thing one human being can do for another.

ELIZABETH EDWARDS

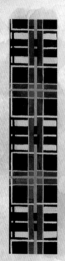

SUMS

In the arithmetic of love, one plus one equals everything, and two minus one equals nothing.

MIGNON MCLAUGHLIN

Once I was one,
Then came you,
Not making two,
'Cos we became one.
Mathematically it
seems,
A bit of a riddle,
For love is quite simply,
Completely illogical.

LINDA MACFARLANE

I would rather have a crust and a tent with you than be a queen of all the world.

ISABEL BURTON
(1831-1896),
TO HER HUSBAND RICHARD

Gladly, I'll live in a poor
mountain hut,
Spin, sew, and till the soil
in any weather,
And wash in the cold
mountain stream, if but
We dwell together.

AUTHOR UNKNOWN

You are a sure holding
in the shifting sands of
life, a certainty that
steadies us and gives
us hope and comfort.

PAM BROWN, B.1928

I once had been lost,
but when I met you
I was found.
You came into my life
and turned my world around.

LISA MARIE NELSON

You have taught me who I am
And what I may become.
You have made new possibilities
spring into life.
You have given meaning
to every day.

PAM BROWN, B.1928

*I look at my husband's
beloved body and I am very
aware of the mystery of
the Word made flesh, his flesh,
the flesh of all of us,
made potential.*

MADELEINE L'ENGLE

To be loved and
chosen by a good man
is the best and sweetest
thing which can happen
to a woman.

LOUISA MAY ALCOTT
(1832-1888),
FROM "LITTLE WOMEN"

He lights my world with love and laughter. He gives to all my days the warm promise of Spring, and because of him I am ever young. So, Darling, for yesterday, today, and all my tomorrows, my love and my thanks.

CATHERINE JENKINSON

He is the one
that makes you feel
like having children
– his children.

DIANE YOUNG

*May heaven grant you in all
things your heart's desire —
husband, house and a happy
peaceful home. For there is
nothing better in this world
than that a man and woman,
sharing the same ideas,
keep house together.*

HOMER (8TH CENTURY B.C.),
FROM "THE ODYSSEY"

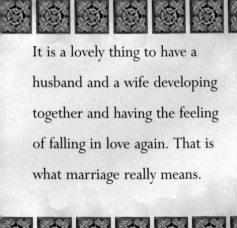

It is a lovely thing to have a husband and a wife developing together and having the feeling of falling in love again. That is what marriage really means.

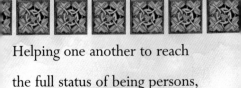

Helping one another to reach
the full status of being persons,
responsible and autonomous
beings who do not run away
from life.

PAUL TOURNIER (1898-1986)

And when we kiss,
a current surges, heart to heart,
carrying all my love to him
and all his love to me.

LINDA MACFARLANE

The little, secret sacred
movements of love between
a man and woman are the
deepest, most mystic things
of life.... I have learned in your
arms the lovely joy of asking
for love, of reaching up
towards you to receive your
love, as if I held myself out
to you....

MARGARET LAWRENCE

A woman knows
the face of the man she loves
as a sailor knows
the open sea.

HONORÉ DE BALZAC (1799-1850)

Constant in a world of change, understanding in a world of indifference, loving and passionate in a world that often hates. He is the sharing of joy and sorrow, the end of loneliness, my lover and the father of my children.

MARION MARSHALL

mis.

You live invisibly in every shared and familiar place, however far away you are.

ng you

When you are away too
long I put on your ancient
gardening jacket and sit
wrapped round in you.

PAM BROWN, B. 1928

I feel

my heart die

a little

Your presence pervades the
house. Even when you are away
I find myself listening for you.
I open doors, half expecting to
find you there, turn to speak
and feel my heart die a little in
the silence. You are in my mind
and in my heart. You are in the
very air I breathe.

ROSANNE AMBROSE-BROWN, B.1943

To lie with you under a ceiling bright with shifting water shadows – that's good. To drowse in flower-scented darkness – that's good. But best of all is rain – brushing quietly against the windows – or drumming, roaring, gushing from the guttering – and we two warm and dry and safe together, in each other's arms.

PAM BROWN, B.1928

I love it that you take the effort to be romantic. That you buy me roses and prepare candlelight dinners complete with champagne. But of all the ingredients that make the perfect romantic evening the one that really matters is you.

LINDA MACFARLANE

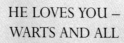

HE LOVES YOU –
WARTS AND ALL

When your hair needs washing;
When you've got a spot on
your chin;
When you have to hold it all
in to get it all in;
A husband is someone who says
"Hey I don't half fancy you."

LINDA E. MACKEY

A husband says "I love you" when you're wearing a face-pack; and remembers your punch-lines for you in public.

JILL WOODS

He's the typical
"no-nonsense",
mustn't show his feelings,
man, who wept
when you refused
his first proposal
of marriage.

JENNY CLEMENTS

POOR GUYS!

Any married man should forget his mistakes. No use two people remembering the same thing.

DUANE DEWEL

HUSBANDS?
Small band of men, armed only
with small wallets, besieged by
a horde of wives and children.

NATIONAL LAMPOON, 1979

He's a chump, you know. That's what I love about him. That and the way his ears wiggle when he gets excited. Chumps always make the best husbands. When you marry, Sally, grab a chump. Tap his forehead first, and if it rings solid, don't hesitate.

P.G. WODEHOUSE (1881-1975)

WOMEN
LIKE SILENT MEN.
THEY THINK THEY
ARE LISTENING.

MARCEL ACHARD

LAZYBONES

Husbands can forget anything
except when to eat.

AUTHOR UNKNOWN,
FROM "TIGERS DON'T EAT GRASS"

He provides honourable
excuses for doing nothing
when household mechanisms
are doing likewise.

J.S. BARBER

Men are like blisters.
They don't show up
until the work is done.

EDWARD PHILLIPS

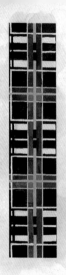

Women speak because they wish to speak, whereas a man speaks only when driven to speech by something outside himself — like, for instance, he can't find any clean socks.

JEAN KERR, B.1923

You can let off steam
to him and rant and
rage, and he'll look
up from his
newspaper and say
"Did you say
something dear?"

ANN WEBB

A VERY ORDINARY MAN...

Statistics prove that the average man today is forty around the waist, ninety-six around the golf course, and a nuisance around the house.

EDWARD PHILLIPS

I never married because there was no need. I have three pets at home which answer the same purpose as a husband. I have a dog which growls every morning, a parrot which swears all afternoon and a cat that comes home late at night.

MARIE CORELLI, FROM "PICKING ON MEN" BY JUDY ALLEN

*A guy is a lump like
a donut. So, first, you
gotta get rid of all the stuff his
mom did to him, and then you
gotta get rid of all that*

macho crap they pick up from
the beer commercials.
And then there's my personal
favorite, the male ego.

ROSEANNE BARR

*In our
very ordinary
lives…*

The astonishing thing is
that, amongst the flotsam
and jetsam of our ordinary
lives, the supermarket
bills, overgrown weeds,
and scraps of food stuck to

last night's dinner plates —
our love remains exotic
and golden and
shimmering, like something
from another world.

SALLY HARRIS

*He's the man who doesn't
have to keep saying
"I love you" because
you know it.
It's written in his eyes.*

LINDA HALL

A husband is a warm cosy glow
that steals over you when you
hear his key in the door, and a
dear liar to boot when he tells
you that you still look as lovely
as you did thirty-five years ago.

LAVINIA MARTIN

HAPPINESS

A happy couple
share a certain smile
that no one else quite
understands.

PAM BROWN, B.1928

Happiness is waking
very slowly and finding
the one you love smiling
at you, watching you
discovering the new day.

CHARLOTTE GRAY, B.1937

LOVE DOESN'T JUST
SIT THERE, LIKE
A STONE, IT HAS TO
BE MADE, LIKE BREAD;
RE-MADE ALL THE
TIME, MADE NEW.

URSULA K. LE GUIN,
B.1929, FROM
"THE LATHE OF HEAVEN"

Some say a husband can't be changed. Untrue. Both partners change in an equal marriage, and he's the man who you finally reach the finishing line with, because he's there beside you, not in front of or behind you.

GILLIAN D.S. WARNER

A successful marriage is not a gift; it is an achievement.

ANN LANDERS, B.1918

A marriage where not only esteem, but passion is kept awake, is, I am convinced, the most perfect state of happiness: but it requires great care to keep this tender plant alive.

FRANCES BROOKE, 1769

TRUST, RESPECT...
A woman should, I think,
love her husband better
than anything on earth
except her own soul, which
I think a man should
respect above everything on
earth but his own soul....

FANNY KEMBLE
(1809-1893)

That quiet mutual gaze of
a trusting husband and wife
is like the first moment of
rest or refuge from a great
weariness or a great danger.

GEORGE ELIOT
(MARY ANN EVANS)
(1819-1880)

Loved and respected by a husband I love and respect, my duties and my pleasures are combined. I am happy, and I ought to be. If there exist more acute pleasures I do not want to know them. Is there a sweeter pleasure than to be at peace

with oneself?... What you call
happiness is but a turmoil of
the senses, a tempest of
passions which it is frightening
to witness even from the safety
of the shore....

CHODERLOS DE LACLOS (1741-1803),
FROM "LES LIAISONS DANGEREUSES"

When you are away I lie alone and listen to the dark, drifting in the patter of the rain, the gusting of the night wind. To be alone does not disturb me, but we are so much a part of one another, my heart still seeks you out when you are gone. I will not trouble you. Only stand most quietly at the edges of your sleep, content to share the night, the rain, the wind with you.

PAM BROWN, B.1928

TIME
APART...

When I reflect tis but eight
daies since we parted, I look
back with wonder; for to me it
seems as many years.

ELIZABETH, LADY BRISTOL,
IN A LETTER TO HER HUSBAND,
JOHN HERVEY, 16 AUGUST 1721

Yet I do not regret that this separation has been, for it is worth no small sacrifice to be thus assured, that instead of weakening, our union has strengthened....

MARY WORDSWORTH,
IN A LETTER TO WILLIAM
WORDSWORTH, 23 MAY 1812

MY BIGGEST BOOSTER

Most closely, I have been aided by my life partner, Martin D. Ginsburg, who has been, since our teenage years, my best friend and biggest booster....

JUSTICE RUTH BADER GINSBURG

It seemed the aim of my husband
to enlighten my reason,
strengthen my judgment, and
give me confidence in my own
powers of mind, which he
estimated more highly than I did.

SARAH JOSEPHA HALE (1788-1879)

LOVELY YEARS

A happy marriage is the best thing life has to offer. It is built up brick by brick over the years and cemented as much by the moments of tenderness as by those of irritation.

JILLY COOPER, B.1937

We have been together for so long we may seem to have come to take each other for granted. We know each other so well we scarcely need to speak. But I know and you know that life together is a constant, quiet astonishment.

PAM BROWN, B.1928

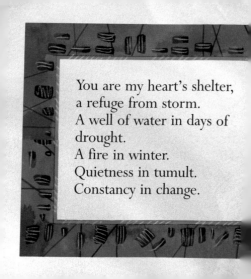

You are my heart's shelter,
a refuge from storm.
A well of water in days of
drought.
A fire in winter.
Quietness in tumult.
Constancy in change.

Sharer of joy.
Companion in sorrow.
Your own being and yet
my other self.
How could I endure
without you?

PAMELA DUGDALE

No, Darling, you're not
absolutely perfect. Thank
goodness. How deadly dull
to be married to a paragon.
Better by far to share my life
with someone human as

myself. Someone who makes
me laugh because we've
passed our sell-by dates.
A friend to turn to, squabble
with and love.

JANE POWELL, B.1942

There is one like him in every woman's life, a man who doesn't quite fit, like a shoe that gives you blisters no matter how hard you try to stretch it. If she's lucky.

EVELYN WILDE MAYERSON, B.1935

Dear ordinary man.
Dear man of little aches and
pains, of aggravating habits,
of quirky laughter. Sometimes of
a sadness I cannot seem to reach.
Dear friend and dear
companion.
Dear enemy. Dear love.
I need you so. Exactly as you are.

PAM BROWN, B.1928

THERE IS NOTHING
MIGHTIER AND NOBLER
THAN WHEN MAN AND WIFE
ARE OF ONE HEART
AND MIND.

HOMER (8TH CENTURY B.C.)

When two people are at one in
their inmost hearts,
They shatter even the strength
of iron or of bronze.
And when two people understand
each other in their inmost hearts,
Their words are sweet and strong,
like the fragrance of orchids.

I CHING

We have changed, you and I.
The mirror says so, and the scales.
And yet in these framed photographs,
Me half-drowned in veiling,
You uneasy in your brand new suit,
We seem unfinished.
I wish I could take their hands,
these two bewildered people, and

tell them what they will become –
that they are only just beginning
the transformation into us:
we two, who have by slow degrees
become so interwoven
we scarcely know
where one life ends
and one begins.

PAM BROWN, B.1928

A MAN IS

NOT WHERE HE LIVES,

BUT WHERE HE LOVES.

LATIN PROVERB

AS THE YEARS ROLL...

I look back to the early days of our
friendship as to the days of love and
innocence, and, with an
indescribable pleasure, I have seen
near a score of years roll over our
heads with an affection heightened
and improved by time.

ABIGAIL ADAMS (1744-1818), TO
JOHN ADAMS, FUTURE PRESIDENT OF
THE UNITED STATES

Love is supposed to start with bells ringing and go downhill from there. But it was the opposite for me. There's an intense connection between us, and as we stayed together, the bells rang louder.

LISA NIEMI

THANK YOU

HOW CAN I COUNT
THE KINDNESS, THE
ASTONISHMENTS, THE JOYS
THAT YOU HAVE GIVEN ME?
YOUR STRENGTH,
YOUR LAUGHTER, THE COMFORT
OF YOUR ARMS.

PAM BROWN, B.1928

You were always there.
No one else was.

HELEN EXLEY

What is a Helen Exley Giftbook?

For 26 years, Helen Exley has created giftbooks, and her
readers have bought 41 million copies of her works.
She dedicates this book to her husband and
business partner, Richard.

Because her books are gifts, Helen makes sure that they
are as thoughtful and meaningful as possible. With infinite
care, Helen Exley ensures that every illustration matches
its quotations, and that the finished book has a depth of
meaning that she can put her name to.

You have the result in your hands.
If you love it – please tell others!

For a full list of Helen Exley's books, write to:

Helen Exley Giftbooks
at 16 Chalk Hill, Watford, WD19 4BG, UK,
or 232 Madison Avenue, Suite 1409, New York,
NY 10016 USA, or visit
www.helenexleygiftbooks.com